Opinionated:
(A Millennial's Memoir) ©
Written By: Joshua Hicks
Cover Art By: Jasmine Ye
Athletes Remorse LLC.
Library of Congress Control Number: 2020910188

Special Thanks:
To my loving family
Bethany Missionary Baptist Church
Tyree Washington
Joshua Brooks
Greg Cross   Michael Garcia
Darius Redmond   Nate Terry   Denis Zimero
Malinda Carlson
Emily Gold   Logan West   Sami Vacek   Nick Tadie
Hannah Baker

Stop!!!

Read.

I was a Black man yesterday, I am a Black man today, and I will be a Black man the day I leave this Earth. When you see me do you see a man? Do you see a monster that society has depicted as public enemy number one? Or do you see just another N (I won't even give you the satisfaction of using that word.) Emotions fuel the body, as rage fuels hatred. In America, it doesn't matter if you committed a crime or not. You see, I was once told you're guilty until you're proven innocent. My coach said that once. The rules change when it wasn't meant for you to win. I see Blacks killed on camera like it's a tv show and the only justice my people can get is a hashtag on a Tuesday. The great Saint Augustine once said "An unjust law is no law at all. Unfortunately, I prefer the late Tupac when he said "I ain't a killer, but don't you push me." As the world around us seems to be collapsing, I want to welcome you to Opinionated: A Millennial's Memoir. Some of you may feel as if you're voiceless, but I promise your voice is stronger than you think. I'm writing this book as a gift to my family and friends, because it is proven that my life can be taken away at any moment. So, I leave you with this, who is Joshua Hicks? Maybe we'll find out together.

Have I not commanded you? Be strong and courageous. Do not be afraid; do not be discouraged, for the Lord your God will be with you wherever you go." Joshua 1:9

Contents

Section 1: Family

Millennial pg.8

Zelda pg.18

Motherless Child pg.19

Mirror Mirror pg.22

Charles pg.23

Corey pg.26

Section 2: Under Construction

Toxic pg.28

11:01 pg.31

Triumphant pg.33

Priority pg.37

Matrimony pg.38

Remorse pg.41

Section 3: PrayingThroughStruggleDaily

PTSD pg.43

Blue Lights pg.46

Mud pg. 52

Redline pg.58

Role Model pg.62

Section 4: Growth

Growth pg.67

Hall Pass pg.70

November pg.79

2020 pg.82

Kobe pg.84

Corona pg.86

Joshua pg.88

Section 1: Family

Millennial

My tongue is my sword, and I assure you I have eviscerated many in my day. – RZA

Growing up in Miami, the only thing a kid wanted to do was play ball, whether it be football or basketball. Unlike some states in Florida, you could start playing the great game of football at age five, but my mom wasn't having that. She didn't want me to be around the park atmosphere where coaches would yell at the players and grown men would place bets on the game. To be blunt, she simply didn't want me getting hurt. This particular year was different. I was nine, I was a big kid, I had big hands, wore size ten shoes and weighed about 150; which is crazy to weigh that much at such a young age, but it wasn't sloppy fat, I was just a big kid. My mom wouldn't let me play at the local parks by the house, so I had to settle for Palmetto Bay park. Which was in a predominantly White area. I was eager because I knew I could dominate. After my paperwork was processed, it was time to step on the scale. According to Pop Warner rules, I was too overweight to play with my age group, and I remember this heavy-set White man approaching me saying: "Son, you need to be playing with the high school boys" and laughed right in my face. I was embarrassed and hurt at the same time because all I wanted to do was play ball. I got back in the car with tears flowing down my face, and with a passionate voice, my mom told me to pick my head up and stated, "Don't let anyone tell you what you can't do and at the end, you'll have the last laugh." And the story begins...

I grew up in a two-parent household with college-educated parents, which meant my margin for error was slim. School was a major emphasis in my house, and I learned early on that education could get me anything I wanted in life or so I thought. Being book smart was a given, but becoming street smart was taught to me from my father. He could sell a Bible to Jesus; that's how good he is, but I'll save him and his story for later. I attended a private Christian school during my elementary years, and that paved the foundation for me. I wish that's all it taught me... but in every kid's life, they reach an age where they understand what race they are. I always knew I was Black, but around the second grade, I started to notice what being Black meant. My classes were still evenly proportioned in grade school, not too many Blacks but not enough to outnumber my White classmates. I could tell you about the time, a teacher accused me of taking a sip out of her soda and how disgusted she was that I could do such a thing; but my mom chewed her out so bad that I believe that poor lady has suffered enough. So instead, let's talk about the 3rd grade Spelling Bee. Now, most of you might think who remembers what happened to them in the 3rd grade, but honestly, I recall that day vividly. We were in the final round, and there five spellers left, and four spellers could advance to regionals. Three participants and an alternate. One of the kids had just misspelled a word and it was my turn. I misspelled my word, and the two kids that spelled their word correctly made the cut, so all my hopes fell in the hands of this girl and her word was "Hawaii." She takes a deep breath and her hands are trembling, I start to grin because in my mind I know she doesn't know it and we'll go to a spell off. She closes her eyes and starts to spell "H-a-w-a-i" my mind goes crazy. She just misspelled it!!! I see my mom in the corner with a sigh of relief. Of course, it's not that easy... just like the infomercials; "But wait there's more!". I'd be damn if the judges announced that the water fountain machine came on and they could not hear whether she spelled the word right or wrong. The room was in an uproar, and the little girl knew JC (Jesus Christ) himself blessed her that day. With her second chance, she spelled the word correctly. I was in so much disbelief I threw the spell off for the alternate spot because in my mind, I was cheated. Most would say I had an opportunity, and I misspelled my word. That's true, but we were kids and coincidently, the Asian and Black students were the ones who had to fight for the last spot. By the time I reached 6th grade, I was ready for a change in pace and decided to attend public school.

My old stomping grounds was Cutler Ridge Middle school. I felt like I was getting baptized when I walked through those gated fences that led me onto the P.E. courts. I went from a school that had about 350 kids to a school that had 1,000 students. My first day reminded me of the movie "The Wood" when Omar Epps's character wanted to slap the girl on her butt. The girls at Cutler Ridge Middle had the mindset of grown women and I was just this chubby kid who could do nothing but smile because I was just happy to see these girls. During lunch, I walked into the boys' bathroom, and a drug deal was going on; this was my first-time seeing weed. My second day, I walked into the same bathroom and they had a full out dice game going on. For most kids, this would've been a turnoff, but for me this was an educational lesson. I learned more things in that bathroom than in the classroom that year. I had the opportunity to be around things that my parents would try to keep me away from. Cutler Ridge Middle made me mentally tough because middle school kids can be some of the most ruthless people you come across. I went from being a chubby kid to a burly young man who smelled good and made all the girls smile.

In the era of skinny jeans, baggy shirts, and pre-cray Kanye West, life was great. Middle school is the most crucial point in a child's life because this is usually the time a kid can go in a positive or negative direction. I never understood why my parents never let me get gold grillz in my mouth, let me sag my pants, or attend house parties in middle school until I got older and I realized they were trying to raise a young man. Not that any of those things could have prevented me from being a man, but it would have given me the mindset that it was okay to be the stereotypical Black man that people perceived to see on television. I had a curfew throughout my high school years. After the football game, I had to go home. I wasn't allowed to go celebrate until 1 or 2 in the morning. Of course, once I became a senior, my leash was loosened and I could go out with my friends, but without even realizing it, I was trained to text my parents and let them know that I was okay, where I was at and who was around me.

I know it was hard for my parents to raise a young Black man in America. I was in the same state where Trayvon Martin was gunned down for having a hoodie on. I was in the same city where King Carter was six years old and was gunned down in a crossfire on his way to buy some candy. Two Black kids dead for just minding their own business. My dad grew up in Louisiana, and my mom was a Black woman, so their overprotectiveness of me was necessary. Growing up Black, you don't necessarily ever have "the talk" with your parents and by talk, I mean the Race talk. It's more so pop quizzes and commandments, or at least that's how it was in my household. "What do you do if you're pulled over by the police?" "Don't ever admit to something you didn't do." Pretty basic things but could easily be forgotten once you're in a situation.

The misinterpretation that many people have who live in Miami is that racism no longer exists or that Florida is not a member of the southern states. Still, once you pass Orlando, the confederate flags start to come out a little more and you begin to have a better understanding of where you're at. During my childhood, it was never in your face racism, but it was little things that happened that I never paid attention too.

At night, I close my eyes like any regular person, but I envision how far I've come in life, yet there's still more out there to accomplish. I am the only child to Larry and Sabrina Hicks. Growing up, I had the best childhood that a kid could have. Both of my parents were in the picture and are happily married. If there were any problems, they made sure never to discuss them in front of me. My mom could brighten a room with her presence and smell alone. With her short haircut and her high fashion style, she always thought she was related to the singer Monica. She was my protector and made sure I never went without. At a young age, my mother and her family had bounced around from school to school and never settled in one place long enough to call it home; but by the time she reached the 8th grade, she was able to attend Palmetto Middle school and later graduate from Miami Southridge Senior High school.

Being one of the smartest people I know, she received her bachelor's and master's degree from Grambling State University, where she met my father. Now, my dad… what can I say about him? Stern, charismatic, family man, and the definition of genuine. My dad is from a small town and grew up during a time where he saw his Black elders refer to their White peers as "Ma'am and Sir". If you're having a hard time grasping this concept, imagine being the same age as someone or maybe even older and you call them by their first name, but society frowns upon you calling a White person by their first name once you're an adult and now you have to call them "Mr. John" as if they're above you. This sticks with a kid, and my father had gone through so much regarding race that his mindset just wouldn't let him ever forget little things like that. He understood that he just couldn't be good at what he did but that he had to be great. He raised a man in me. Lord knows he was tough on me, and at times I couldn't understand why, but as I get older, I see.

Zelda

I've named the subtheme of this chapter, "Zelda." Zelda Hicks was my aunt who passed away a few years ago. She was something else, but she loved her family and I can personally admit she was one of my favorite people to talk to. I speak of women highly because all the women in my family are strong independent Black women. So, this chapter is necessary because when I lost this lady a piece of me left because she was one of my biggest supporters. I never grieved the way I needed too because she left behind two sons, and if it were killing me with her absence, I couldn't even walk in the shoes of my cousins. It's often asked how Black men cope with their feelings? The answer is simple, we don't. It may be unfair for me to answer that fairly, so I try to put my thoughts on paper hoping it would have the same effect on him. I decided to let my cousin speak his mind, so with this I introduce the world to Darian Watson.

Dear Motherless Child

I know things are rough in the beginning and it can all be confusing. Thoughts such as "Why it'd have to be me" start to surface. Your emotions get distorted and at times you may even question your own existence. To others, it seems like you're just mad at the world, but the truth is you get highly upset or frustrated because you don't understand it all. The pain never seems to go away, and it looks like your mind may never find peace because as you look around, even the slightest things seem to remind you of your mother. But it would help if you viewed it as though they're now at peace. Instead of feeling sorrow for yourself, you should feel joy for the one that has passed over. For they no longer have to feel pain and their days of suffering are now over.

Don't allow yourself to drown in depression or shut yourself away from the world. You may need time alone to allow yourself to accept the loss and progress past it fully, but don't shut out or turn away people that genuinely care about you or that are willing to help you through it. Even the strongest of people need someone to lean on in hard times, so don't feel weak for seeking help. I know you feel as though nobody truly understands your pain or how you feel, so you may think that it's pointless to have those conversations with people, but just being able to vent and let some of those emotions out will ease your mind.

A wise person once said, "Let your pain be worth something." So, I say let your situation be your motivation. Your situation doesn't define you; you define yourself. Don't let the loss of your loved one become an excuse for anything negative you may do. Everyone goes through things but not everyone makes it out. It's bittersweet in a sense. While on one side it hurts you, it gives you a push in life. It forces you to be a better you because now you have no choice but to stand on your own two feet and be a man/woman. It should give you the motivation to keep progressing in life. Just because she lost her life, doesn't mean yours should stop. Keep pushing yourself and don't give up until you accomplished something amazing, because everyone knows mothers love to see their baby doing great things.

Life brings about many different obstacles. Only 10% of it is what happens to you; the other 90% is how you react to it.

Mirror Mirror

Sometimes we carry the burden of being mistreated by previous loved ones. Not everyone is upset with you, annoyed with, or wishing on your downfall. I just want you to know your presence alone is enough and much appreciated. You're the full package, so always grant yourself the same respect you give others.

Charles

If you ever ask a young boy what would be the first thing they would buy if they became rich? I can bet most would say: "I'm going to buy my mom a house or car." It's an instinct to take care of the woman who raised you. Often these young boys are athletes and believe it or not; we all think we're going to make it out. You see, everyone has that one story or person that pushes them to be better. My person just so happens to be named Charles.

Legendary... this nine-letter word is what my dad described to me the day before my high school State championship game. He stated that people remember greatness, but legends live forever.
Before Friday Night Lights the movie and Boobie Miles, there was Charles Andrews and the Jonesboro-Hodge Tigers. Although I never saw him play, to sum it all up, Charles was poetry in motion on the football field. A member of the 1987 National Champion NLU Indians (now ULM Warhawks), he was destined for

legendary status. My father and Charles were two peas in a pod. Charles was an underclassman at NLU, and number 14 was taken, so he wore the number of his best friend. The legendary number 4. After winning the national championship, Charles started suffering excruciating headaches. Shortly after, Charles suffered a brain aneurysm, ending his dreams of the NFL.

(Enters park legend)

The park legend is someone everyone knows in the neighborhood. The prodigy that everyone yells, "Don't forget about me when you make it," but life happens, and this once prized athlete is forgotten. Society has a weird way of respecting legends, right? The once gifted basketball player who went to a party and got his drink spiked is now the guy who plays shadow ball in the park by himself. The kids laugh because he's dribbling without a ball; the truth is, this guy is playing against himself because, at one point, the only person who could stop him was himself.

Sometimes we mistake what legendary can mean to certain people; because whether they know it or not, my father and Charles showed me that even friendships could be legendary. When I see Charles today, I don't see him in a wheelchair. I imagine him as the guy who used to leave people on their feet, wondering what he will do next. When I see Charles, I smile and can't help but think, "Momma, there goes that man!

Corey

Dear Corey,

It's been a while… To think that you're gone still seems unreal, even if it has been six years. You made an impact on people and you didn't even know it. You were a great teammate and an even better friend. I couldn't find the strength to make the funeral but seeing you in a casket wasn't the lasting memory I wanted of you. As men we're taught to not show emotion, so I buried it as far in my conscious as I could. Believe it or not Greg and I finally got playing time just like we always said we would during our freshman year. I was named team captain, but Greg; he'll be an IC Hall of Famer. I hope we made you proud, my brother. We miss you, but more importantly we love you.

RIP Corey Moore

Section 2: Under Construction

Toxic

Interesting title to name this segment, but maybe towards the end, you'll understand the meaning behind it. In life, things come full circle; some call it karma others say its life. Opinionated: A Millennial's memoir is the title, but this right here is the testimony. Pastor Williams says it best, "I promise not to keep you too long." A year can change your life and in my case it did. I've been blessed, but sometimes you still don't know what your purpose in life is. People tell you that they're proud of you, and that can be the best feeling in the world, but at the same time, it creates this boulder on your shoulders that you can't let people down. I will give the shirt off my back if it's someone I care about; so, the last thing I would want to do is disappoint. Built from a different cloth, everyone I surround myself around is strictly positivity. You lose people in your life that you once broke bread and cried with. Understand, not everyone is in your corner.

Recognize that people in your life have seasons. Don't worry; this isn't a wellness book of any sort. I want you all to understand that everyone highlights their wins, but few acknowledge their losses. I've lost a few people in my life, whether it was to an unfortunate circumstance, or their season had ended. We can't save everyone, and realistically you shouldn't because when you win, everyone wants that piece, but when you lose, you're taking that L on the chin. Perfection is intangible and striving for the world everyone else wants for you will leave you feeling empty.

One of the greatest things in life that a person can do is reflect. Twenty-four years young and I can proudly say that I'm not the man I thought I would be. Being so young, I believed being married and having a child right now would be living lavish. Reality is I'm single and still figuring things out. I asked one of my brothers one night, "do you believe God is punishing us because he sent us our wife in college, and we stood her up; and now he's making us learn the hard way?" He chuckled and replied, "N*gga, what?" Then proceeded to ask me if I thought I was successful? If I ran down my accomplishments, so far, I'm successful. I'm not rich, but I afford the little things. Even with that being said, I still think I'm struggling with PTBD (Post-traumatic Black Disorder). Is that a thing?

11:01

Hey, it's me again...

It's been some time since we last spoke, but I knew you would be here to listen

Remember when you used to have dreams of playing in the league and being rich?

Or back when kid cuisine and cartoons filled up the school nights.

[(Chuckles)]

You see, I had nobody else to turn to and I knew you would be there for me

There's this burden that I can't seem to shake and every time I run; you pop up

I guess I can't avoid you.

In all honesty, I'm afraid of success and what if the world doesn't like what I have to say?

Young, Black, and educated. If it's not me, then who?

If you were in my shoes, you would know what to do

Sometimes you must remind yourself

That's why I wrote this letter to myself...

TRiUMPhant!

I don't scratch my head unless it itches, and I don't dance unless I hear music.

-Denzel Washington (Remember the Titans)

Let me take you back to a story I was once told titled "Purple Turkey". One day, this young girl in kindergarten was in class, coloring a turkey for Thanksgiving. Most kids in the class painted their turkey brown, but this young girl decided to color hers purple. The class laughed, and the teacher was puzzled and asked the little girl why did she color her turkey purple? This young child painted her turkey purple because when she had seen one beforehand, she saw how beautiful its tail was and when it reflected off the sun, the feathers were purple. I told you this story because why does it matter what color a 5-year-old colors a turkey? Why not allow people to use their imagination? The number one reason why dreams do not come true is that we grow old, and we let society stop us from using our imaginations. The world is collapsing around us daily, and the only positivity one can have is their peace of mind. What happened to wanting to be a superhero? Don't misquote me; I'm not encouraging anyone to jump in chemical waste in hopes of gaining powers, but why not want to be a superhero to your kids or friends and just life in general?

The US Women's national soccer team is a group that I believe are national heroes. They represent everything that is America; don't believe me? Let's check the qualifications of what makes Americans think someone is a national treasure:

1. **Diversity**: This is a crucial component because this team was made up of women from different races, sexual orientations, socioeconomic backgrounds (They don't get equal pay, so it's not much).

2. **Freedom of speech**: That is every American's favorite Amendment, mainly because that's the only one people remember. Just like the 45th President, these women say what is on their mind.

3. **Equality**: This might be one of my favorites because if you thought you were going to only give these women a 9 million dollar cut after winning the World Cup, please rethink that mentality.
4. **Winners**: I couldn't forget about this vital qualification. This group of women are winners and every American loves a winner. I'm not talking about winners like in the Marvel superhero movies where the hero gets defeated in the first hour of the film and magically comes back and wins in the end. No, these ladies win like a fifteen-year old playing in a ten-year old AAU basketball division; it's not even close.
5. **Patriotic**: The thirteen colonies had the Boston Tea Party, and 2019 was blessed with Alex Morgan sipping her tea after a goal.

Now that I made my brief presentation on why these women are heroes let's discuss ourselves and how we all can be heroes.

This chapter is titled triumphant, yet there are many directions I can take this chapter. When I think of triumphant, this gut feeling tells me to take my time on this one and open up. The glue to a family will always be the mother, and in most cases, it's because she will sacrifice the most to ensure her family's needs are met. It's a sensitive topic, but it's overdue. Women are no longer taking the backseat to men. If you're old enough, you can relate to the little catchy song that goes, "Anything you can do, I can do better." Well we men knew women could probably do things better, but ego is a tricky trait to have. Young women in this generation are attending college and working in professions that don't require them to be a stay at home mom. Special shout-out to those women working at Hooters and strip clubs putting that money towards a better lifestyle. We look down on them too much. I would be a hypocrite if I didn't say my friends and I didn't donate a few dollars to these women's lifestyle.

__Priority__

In life we're our biggest critics. We want to be loved without loving ourselves.

We want people to accept us but have no idea what we're even offering them.

I understand that in life, love comes and goes. While heartbreak has remained consistent.

Friends have turned their backs. You pray for them while they have preyed on you.

Yet, through adversity you push through.

Matrimony

She said you don't know how good it is to be you because you're him.

-Drake

If you ever get the opportunity to ask a group of young people what their opinion on marriage is you will receive a million different responses. To even get to the marriage question you first have to present the question of "Do you believe in love?" To the curious mind, most say they do. In society today, there are so many distractions; how does one stay on the straight path of commitment without sliding into the DM's? Let's lay the cards on the table and play the game of love. We're a few months into dating and you want me to trust you, but you don't trust me. That's strike one. Social media is like quicksand and if you move too much, you will get sucked in. It doesn't matter how old you are, once a new relationship is formed most couples run to social media to announce the news. We're excited for your happiness, but now you have invited the world into your relationship. Although you have a crowd of support, there are some who are hoping you two don't make it.

If social media is a black hole, then Instagram is the sunken place for relationships. One double tap or DM can test the strongest of relationships. Instagram is the one platform where you can live a life that nobody else would even know about. There's a lot of people you come across their page and sometimes you have to second guess your life decisions. You have your self -proclaimed millionaires, women who bought a camera off Amazon and are now Instagram models, and then you have your pop tart couples (as I like to call them.), I call them that because as quick as they're hot, they turn cold. Depending on the day you'll see them at Disney World and the next day, one of them is in someone else's DM's telling you that they're on a break. Let's call a spade a spade, this makes dating hard nowadays. DMX said it best "It's hard staying sucka free in a world full of lollipops"; depict that how you want but it makes sense to me. As loyal as you may want to believe someone is, it might lead to heartbreak.

Some may wonder if I even believe in love and the answer is yes, but maybe not in the ways you may think. You just can't be closed minded and say you're in love with a person because of looks, wealth, or even sex. I can't fill that void for a woman who has "daddy issues" and vice versa for a person who deals with a man who is too clingy. It's unrealistic to sit here and have a job description of the perfect partner, but when I find her, I'll be sure to include that in a book.

Remorse

I was 19 years-old the first time I thought about marriage.

You looked at me, I looked at you, and the rest was perfect like an Illinois sunset.

Like most, it was iconic how we met.

But I ended up being just like the rest.

Spent more time asking who and where?

Instead of questioning was love really in the air.

Was it lust?

Or was I more concerned when I could get that last bust?

As you walk down the aisle

I can do nothing but smile

Maybe it's from feeling sympathy

Or I'm just grateful it isn't with me.

Section 3: PTSD (Praying Through Struggle Daily)

Praying **T**hrough **S**truggle **D**aily

It's beauty in the struggle, ugliness in the success.

Love Yourz J. Cole

August 12th, 2018, this is the day I got baptized or reborn, whichever is the proper term. I was always a praying man and came from a religious family. Didn't go to church every Sunday until I was twenty-three and lived with my Godfather, who said there are two rules in his house; "You go to school and you go to church." If I had a choice right then and there, I would have moved back to Miami. Going to school wasn't the issue, and church wouldn't have been a problem, if I didn't live in Louisiana where church lasted two-plus hours. Then this crazy thing happened, and I ended up loving church. I didn't know if it was because I was older and mature enough to handle the message, or the Lord was working overtime on me. It's like listening to J. Cole and understanding his lyrics because you emotionally understand the picture he's painting; or watching a Jordan Peele movie, and you got the concept after watching "US" once. Prayer became my best friend in 2019 because I needed guidance to prepare me for the path I was on.

As I grow older, I notice more things that used to be relevant to me not matter as much as they used too. Having that dream job starts to fade away because priorities begin to pile up. Getting married and having kids is looking like an alternate universe because the reality you're living is showing you that social media relevance is more valuable than spending time with the person you love. A 30-second video can make you famous and leave someone who's been acting their whole life without a movie role. Back in the day, most people used to pack their bags and move to LA and New York City to chase their dreams; now, people move to facilitate a lifestyle that looks like a college girl's refrigerator, cold and empty. Parents spend $5k on prom for a kid who is getting a certificate of completion. Too far! I apologize, because like everything else millennials are entitled because our parents raised us that way, but those Baby Boomers won't get off our backs and think that the thing called WIFI has ruined us.

Blue Lights

Neither slavery nor involuntary servitude, except as a punishment for crime whereof the party shall have been duly convicted, shall exist within the United States, or any place subject to their jurisdiction.

-United States 13th Amendment

Know your rights… if you don't understand what I mean, read the sentence above one more time and try to grasp the concept that the United States Constitution is a set up for a person to belong to the system forever. In 1865 slavery was abolished in the United States of America, but the thirteenth Amendment in lesser terms is an escape route to enslave the people once again. No man or woman will be a slave unless they commit a crime and are found guilty and will be a slave to the State of where they are being imprisoned. One mistake can ruin your life forever. I can't lie to you; as a young Black man, I'm terrified that being at the wrong place at the wrong time can be it for me. You can be an outstanding family man, a God-fearing man, and a graduate from Harvard, but handcuffs don't discriminate against people who look like me. (Here we go another Black Lives Matter rant) if that were true, a rant would be an understatement for this segment.

In my short time on Earth, I have gone back and forth with liking and disliking police officers. I lived with one for a year, and he's a damn good one. History tells us you're supposed to hate the cops, pigs, 12, opps, whatever street name you have for them. They stop us for no reason, mess up our parties, they harass and kill people who look just like me! A White man can go into a school and shoot it up and walks out bullet free. A Black man who is in his backyard can be gunned down for no apparent reason but for walking while Black. I always try to be optimistic, but every now and then, I must be ignorant.

Although, everyone has their reasons for liking or disliking police officers; the inner me is forever grateful for the men and women who risk their lives to protect and serve. These officers are some of the people who made the most significant impact on your life. These officers removed from the badge, are coaches, parents, pastors, and barbers. It's a touchy subject, and if you're not ready to see how in-depth this chapter goes, I understand.

Digging deep into my memory box. One night, my friends and I were coming back from a party, music was blasting, an open bottle of alcohol in the car, and some smelling like weed. We make a right, and this officer gets behind us, we make another turn, and the unit is right on our tail. We turned the music down; we start discussing what we should do if we get pulled over. The heart starts beating faster; paranoia is a b**ch. That night we didn't get pulled over. Just like most college kids, we were being dumb and shouldn't have had an open bottle in the car, but at that moment, I couldn't help but see my friend's faces, but even worse I saw the shame. This shame wasn't because of us being careless, it came from fear. We all had the same thought process of, we were screwed if we got pulled over. Five Black men in Jacksonville,

Illinois. I don't even want to think about what could have happened. I went back and saw how far we were from campus when we made that drive. It was half a mile; God is good all the time.

6x8

You have the right to remain silent. Anything you say can and will be used against you in a court of law. Any person who has ever seen a crime movie or show knows the Miranda rights. They say prison is as close to hell as you can get before actual death itself. To be locked in a cage 23 hours out of 24 can make anyone lose their mind. Some of those people deserve it. To be honest, the right amount deserves it. There are levels to this madness, though; don't say free (Insert street name here), and that person robbed a house and shot everyone in it down to the sheepdog. That person deserves to be in there but locking someone up for weed, and this person isn't pushing significant weight; for example, it's a person who's been selling dime bags since high school and ten years later they are just now selling a zip. Why even consider throwing that person in jail for years when they just wasted a decade on $150 profit.

In eighth grade, I was a member of 5000 Role Models, which is an organization that mentors young minority men for the real world. On this one field trip, they took us to the prison, somewhat a scared straight program. Ten prisoners were presented, nine were Black men, four were ex-college football players, none attained a college degree. You can watch "Beyond Scared Straight" on television, but it's the opposite. Some guys try to intimidate you, but when you listen to their stories, they preach to you to stay in school and don't become another statistic. Every year on my birthday, I have a checklist I go through: the first point is, I survived another year (I'm sorry I lived another year), point two is I'm still earning an education. My last point is, I have never been arrested a day in my life.

Some may laugh at that last point, but when a system is strategically created for you to fail, it's a lot harder to accomplish that last point. 6x8 is the average size of a prison cell give or take. It is created to help one rehabilitate him or herself of the crime they have committed. The cell is a physical representation, but your mind is the real prison. The prison system is the modern-day Willie Lynch. Prisoners work hard labor hours for a pack of Ramen noodles at the end of the week. Keep the body strong! But keep the mind psychologically weak!

Great leaders have emerged from prison because they kept their minds strong. It doesn't matter if you're locked away or in the free world; individuals will test you daily to take away your mind. So, I guess the real question is, will you let them?

Mud

Y'all rooting for me but are y'all really rooting for me. Bobby Bruce
(Last Chance U)

Today we like to use the phrase "got it out the **mud**," which indicates we started from the bottom or nothing to reach success. Now being 24 and it being a year removed from "College Uncensored", life is looking up for me. I now have my master's degree from "**The**" Grambling State University, have a car, and started my own company, "Athletes Remorse Publishing." Yet, there is still more out in the world to achieve. Through selling my first book, I saw a lot of people who supported me, but I needed to cut the grass a little lower to fully understand that snakes wished for my downfall. Even Amazon was trying to sabotage the listing price on my book to ensure that I would sign with their publishing company. Success doesn't come overnight, especially in my case…

During my freshman year of high school, I was cut twice from the JV football team. We had over 150 kids trying out to play junior varsity football, and I always struggled with separating myself from the pack when it came to sports. I was devastated when I first got the news that I didn't make it. My mom picked me up, and I told her the story. Now, let me remind you that my mom never played sports so she couldn't attain the concept of me being cut. She told me that maybe I overlooked my name and should recheck the list. Foolishly, I rechecked the list, and just like I thought, my name was not on it. At the time, my cousin was supposed to be the next big thing at the school, so his dad pulled a few strings with the varsity coach, and I was able to stay on the team. Life is never that easy… less than 18 hours later I would receive the news I did not make the final roster. This was like a bad episode of NFL Hardknocks. A few days pass, and the house phone was ringing, it was my mom, and she was excited to tell me that the Junior Varsity Head coach had requested me to play on the team because he didn't like to cut freshman. So that following week I was a JV football player. I had a helmet that was too small for my head and shoulder pads that had straps that would break off every time someone hit me. When it came to game time, I had to wear a practice jersey because we didn't have enough game jerseys. Humble beginnings for sure, but more obstacles were to come. After football season, it was time for basketball, and that was my main love. Different sport same result, except this time I was on the team with a few exceptions. I had all the responsibilities of a team manager and a player. If washing your teammate's jerseys doesn't give you a slice of humble pie, nothing will. This was the lowest point of my life. I was unhappy for sure and wanted to throw a pity party every day, but my dad stepped in and said these exact words, "You going to pout every day, or are you going to change the outcome?"

Fast forward, in high school, I became a two-sport captain, a starter on the football team, and helped win the school's first football

State Championship. I got to college and became a starter and was selected by my peers to be a team captain. I was never the best player, but I always wanted to be the best teammate. Forget my stats; what did we do as a team. Did my teammates feel welcomed by me? Now that's getting it out the mud. In life, we'll be hit with different obstacles, but we can always rewrite the ending. My parents were my core and pushed me to be motivated. Coach Elliot gave me an opportunity to play on his JV football team along with Coach Bundy. Coach Corbett named me a captain and let me know I was the right man for the job. Coach K taught me adversity and later rewarded me with being captain. I got to college and was the first Black offensive lineman to start for the school in over ten plus years. I was humble in the first book, but if you want facts, those are some for your ass.

Participation Trophy

I don't know when this started, but seeing young kids getting rewarded for everything is destroying upcoming generations' sense of hard work. Let me rephrase that; it began in my generation as much as I would like to deny it. In elementary, I could remember having the end of the year ceremonies, and you'll have the honor roll students which was expected then you would have most improve, which is fair for a student who was struggling and ended up doing well towards the end. Then teachers started getting creative because you have those kids who fall in between and qualify for neither. This puts a teacher in an awkward position because parents begin to complain. In the fifth grade, it got out of hand; I received the "A" honor roll and Most honest award. That was their way of saying I said whatever came to my mind, and I guess it held up because I won most opinionated in high school with a population of 4,000 students, so you know I was blunt and to the point.

We use failure as a crutch and don't teach kids how to overcome adversity. College athletics has the transfer portal where a student-athlete can enter their name in the transfer portal and go to any college they want if things don't work out at the previous school. This has now become a part of high school sports. Miami-Dade County alone has accepted this trend to the fullest effect. A student can play football at one school in the Fall and be playing basketball in the Winter at another school. Instant success!! But it's only a quick fix for a scenario that you'll have in the real world.

Not everyone can be number one, but that doesn't mean you can't be the best version of yourself...

Redline

"Where you going ain't on the map" – Rev. Lavell Warren

Gentrification is spreading rapidly across our country like wildfire, and for my readers who don't understand what gentrification is, here are a few examples. If you're from Miami-Dade County, remember when Carol City turned into Miami Gardens, or Cutler Ridge became Cutler Bay. These cities are now incorporated, and all this means is a group of wealthy people bought up a bunch of property for cheap. It made the city look nice to kick out the previous population to move in a group of up and coming business-minded millennials who will pay a ridiculous amount of money to stay in an apartment complex that was once home to drug dealers and low-income families. Redline now comes into play. Redline in the business world means to refuse a loan or insurance to someone because they live in an area deemed to be a reduced financial risk (thank you, New Oxford Dictionary). You see, when they say reduced financial risk, they are referring to the "projects, ghetto, slums, section 8, the trap". It has many different names but equals one thing, poor people. For years America has been built on stolen opportunities. It started with tricking the Native Americans out of their land; then, it led to taking the mindset of Blacks. Willie Lynch is an old American folk story to intimidate the minds of Black slaves. The story goes that Southern White plantation owners were struggling to control their Black slaves, so they sent for a vicious slave owner from the West Indies by the name of Willie Lynch. He came and taught them his methods; the word lynching is derived from his name. His goal was simple: take the mind and leave the body. Keep the mind of a slave psychologically weak so that they can only depend on their slave master but keep the body strong so that they will always get the job done. It's 2020, yet my people and I are still trying to gain control of our minds. Gentrification would be a great thing if we weren't driving the people out who originally lived there. Rebuild these schools and housing complexes, bring healthy food options to the neighborhood, but keep the people involved. The City of Oakland is pretty much gone; it's almost like when the Golden State Warriors became good, the city was lost. Understand that I'm not against the rebuilding of underprivileged neighborhoods. Still, I am skeptical of the idea that the only areas that are getting special treatment are the ones that draw interest from the wealthy. Movies and television shows document gentrification at its finest. Brooklyn is no longer the same place that was home to hip-hop's most famous that drew inspiration for many. Change doesn't always mean eviction.

Zone 4

Jonesboro, Louisiana, is my sanctuary and my place of refuge. College Uncensored was written in this small town of Louisiana. This place was pivotal in my growth as a man. Life lessons here motivated me to be better, and if you took a snapshot of Jonesboro today, you would think the photo was taken in the 1990s. If cities are being gentrified, this is one town that got left behind. A city that has so much history and pride is just one of the many places that don't make the cut of evolving. Jonesboro reminds me a lot of Florida City, FL. Two areas that have a sense of pride but don't have the same resources as cities around them. The 45th President says Make America Great Again; I say Make America equal. Trump stated in one of his speeches that Americans need a side hustle to go along with their jobs in order to have a stable income. He said the obvious because everyone I know has a side hustle. What would you do if you were in a situation to change the people's lives around you? Would you grab your stuff and leave like most, or would you buy the block back?

Role Model

In most urban communities, there are few outlets of positive role models, or maybe it is brainwashed in our minds. There's the local barber who everyone goes to for a haircut and usually receives advice from; he makes good quick money. You have the neighborhood coach who has helped mold future professional athletes but never gets a dime but a "thanks coach." Whether you're a schoolteacher, in law enforcement, or handyman, they each are respectable occupations. Still, none will ever reach the same glamour as being a professional athlete, rapper, or drug dealer. And yes, I said, "DRUG DEALER." It's not a path that most want to go down, but at times this is what influences us as minorities. The pipeline from the schoolhouse to jailhouse is a real thing, and we've been led astray to think anything different. I always see posts on social media of everyone reposting friends and neighborhood stars that make it in the league. Even Soundcloud rappers have a strong following when it comes to support in their music. When "College Uncensored" was first published, I had to understand that what I was doing hadn't been done within my age group or community. As a kid, it's proven that with hard work, you could make it to the league, or with the right beat, you could become a rapper. These were a million to one odds but could be attained. You see, I went on the path that was less taken and might not ever see millions in my account; it' a small sacrifice to teach young ones to dream again. In the time we're living in, anything is possible.

The most challenging thing for me growing up was finding out my dad was a regular person. As random as it sounds, we grow up believing our fathers are these invincible humans that have nothing that can hurt them. I've never seen my father cry; I heard him once. I guess he thought everyone was asleep and it was just him. It wasn't for very long, but in that one instance, I recognized he hurts too. He always preached to me that I could lose him, and it will hurt, but losing my mom would be a completely different hurt.

A poll taken by the Census Bureau in 2016 stated that 69 percent of Black children under the age of 18 grew up in a two-parent household. Now, television has a tricky way of portraying things because most times, they love to focus on Blacks coming from a single-parent home, and we the people sit there and believe that this is normal. Thursday, June 20th, 2019, was the NBA draft. This night stood out to me the most; sure, there was great talent all around, but this night I saw several Black fathers with their sons on draft day. These weren't your cliché Black fathers who only show up on draft day, but these were men that played significant roles in their son's lives. The Center for Disease Control (CDC) stated Black fathers are more likely than their White and Hispanic counterparts to feed, eat with, bathe, diaper, dress, play with and read daily to their children. Now, it would be crazy if I was trying to imply that Black fathers are better because that's not what I'm suggesting; I am stating that let's delete this narrative of Black fathers being absent. I see young Black fathers like Greg Cross,

Nate Terry, Keyno Richardson, and Kenny Lloyd; I praise them because they're doing it the right way.

Section 4: Growth

Growth

In a time where there is so much money to be made, I think the only thing that irritates me more is unmotivated people. You see, most people have these pipe dreams of becoming successful and having generational wealth and whatever else is the norm for a millennial trying to explain to their parents why they haven't found a job yet. There are the rappers, the real estate agents, podcasters/writers (myself) and the pyramid scheme business folks who try to sell you stuff and never held a conversation with you. The honest truth is most young adults nowadays just don't want to work for someone and report to a 9-5 job that we may have seen our parents do for 30 years. It scares us to end up doing something we're not passionate about and I'm one of those people, but this is where things get interesting. If you scroll down your newsfeed whether it's Facebook or Instagram, I guarantee there is at least one person running a business trying to promote something. It can be music, a book, jewelry, health products, the list goes on.

Now, the moment of truth happens and when you find out what you are really made of. When a person finally decides to let the world know what their passion is; you need a core group. Your core group just can't be a bunch of yes men/women who say everything you do is awesome. That's unrealistic and you're cheating yourself. We all need a person who will tell you "Fuck your dreams" as Charlamagne Tha God would say. This person isn't harsh or a hater they just tell you how it is. I had a woman once tell me, "I see people buying your book and I'm sure it's good, but you never talked to me a day in your life and you expect me to buy your book?" The emotion in me boiled up and I wanted to chew her out. For what? Because she told me the truth? Right then and there I could have quit, that's what an unmotivated person would have done.

Instead it was time to reflect and grow as a person. I realized I needed to start networking with more people rather than just ask people to buy from me. I'm not one to tell someone to stop pursuing their dreams, but you must invest in your craft and stop comparing yourself to others. Whether people know it or not, growth is an emotion. You can't know your future if you haven't accepted the past.

Hall Pass

It takes a village to raise a child. – African Proverb

As I sit in the library writing this chapter, I see a mother with her children, homeschooling them. Growing up there were almost no kids that I knew of that were being homeschooled, but in 2019 it's a more recurring theme. She has them in their little study areas, and each is working.

We preach it; we love it, hell I wrote a book on it. I always reminiscence back to school because of my short twenty-four years on this Earth, I've been in school for twenty-one of those years. Most people don't get to see the things I have at the institutions I attended. One thing always remained consistent for me, and that was the number of Black educators I had in my life. I can count on my fingers all of the Black educators I had in school; some may think it's a bad thing, but I see it in a positive light because each of these teachers helped mold me into the man I am today.

Miss Glass was my first-grade teacher. Average height, medium-length black hair, silky chocolate complexion with glasses, by far one of my favorites. Although we were just in the first grade, she had expectations of us as one would have for a third-grade class. If you haven't taught in a classroom, then you wouldn't understand that there's a big difference between third graders and first graders. Miss Glass taught me how to tie my shoes. She made me take this Ked shoe home to practice, and each morning I was tasked with tying the shoelaces. Sounds simple enough, right? If you ask my mom, she will tell you I'm a man of many talents, but my motor skills are downright pitiful. Miss Glass didn't give up on me though, and eventually I got it. I loved that class.

Oddly enough, I didn't have my next Black teacher until middle school, Mrs. Parker's English class. She was stern, but she was a cool lady. We had to write a lot in this class, and I discovered that I had a passion for writing. I apologize for my friends and I saying, "Mrs. Parker when you going to let me f*ck". You have to understand we were young, and the movie Friday is a classic movie with an even more famous line, so when you have a teacher named Mrs. Parker you have to take advantage.

Miss Ruffin of South Dade Senior High school, I don't know where you're at now, but I want to say thank you. You were by far the hardest teacher I had ever taken. I was terrified of math and still am. I would walk into your class, and you would say "Little Black boy," and I couldn't do anything but smile. You were a blessing to my peers and me. You were hard on us, especially to the Black kids, but that's because you knew it was your right too! You knew the world was a cold-hearted place for us, and if we could get through your class, no other teacher/professor could break us.

To my GramFam staff at The Grambling State University, you all taught me life situations and how to carry myself in a manner that everyone notices when I walk into a room. It was only a year, but it was the most enjoyable year of my life.

Signature

I'm a schoolboy, and I can't even deny it. The art of learning motivates me to be great, and in most cases, I feel the need that I must attain these degrees. It was always around me; everyone in my family has either attended college or graduated from college apart from maybe two or three. Do I believe college is necessary? It depends on the day and individual. The ability to read and write is my privilege as an American citizen. My great-great-grandmother was born in 1910; she went her whole life, not being able to read nor write; she would sign her name with the letter x. My people were forced to use old textbooks and weren't allowed to get the same education as their White peers. My people had to create their own college institutions. I'm not asking for compassion; I'm reflecting on excellence at its finest. One hundred years ago, my great- great grandmother couldn't read or write, and her great-granddaughter and great-great-grandson have attained multiple college degrees. I wear that honor with pride.

They have taken cursive writing out of public schools, and children don't even know how to sign their name; reading is at a low because there's this thing called an audiobook that reads for you. Yet, there's always hope because look at you! You've read this far into my book, and there's no audiobook version. Maybe one day, just not today.

John Hancock, do you know him? Or anything that he has done? I guarantee most of you who do identify him relate to his big ass signature on the Declaration of Independence. Some question why he would sign it that big but let's be realistic; he did it to separate himself from others, your name is who you are, it's what makes you different, but your signature tells your story. When ink hits the paper, it leaves a mark. When you sign your name, it signifies who you are.

Mr. Hicks

Never in my life would I have thought I was going to be a teacher in the public-school system, but life throws you curveballs, and I think Justin Verlander (*Major League Baseball player*) was on the mound when this position came open for me. I talk about different generations throughout the book, but this younger generation, who was born in 2003-2010, has me completely lost. I've never felt old until I became a teacher. I go to bed at 9:30 pm and every Friday, I have this urge to go out with other teachers to Chili's and go to happy hour to talk about how bad these kids are. It's a blessing, because so many of us talk about these kids and how they are raised and never take an opportunity to teach them right from wrong. Some of these kids can care less, but many are looking for guidance.

I see bright futures in many of them; they just lack maturity. When it comes to common sense, it doesn't exist for them, but when it comes to being innovative, I can't help but be a little jealous that they know so much more about technology than I did growing up. Although 90's kids can go in either direction, we still get grouped with 2000's babies and how we are self-entitled and lazy. Those two might be accurate, but at least we're not the kids eating Tide pods for fun. By the time I was nine years old, I had my own cell phone. The most basic phone a person could have, but it was mine. Now there are kindergarten children with the latest iPhone. We honestly can't blame parents for this because technology is continuously evolving around us. The issue comes that we have become so attached to technology that we can't getaway. I'll be the first to admit that I go everywhere with my phone and if I don't have it, I'm in trouble. My college roommates could play video games nonstop without ever leaving the sticks. Young women will watch Netflix repeatedly while Siri and Alexa have become the most popular women in a household since Playboy magazine. But for every blessing, there's a curse and the nagging curse happens to be social media. Facebook, Snapchat, Twitter, etc. We have single-handedly brainwashed society to think and act a certain way. Once you post something, it will never go away. Unfortunately, what someone wrote at age 14 could follow them when they're 23, but it happens.

Many young children no longer learn from there households as much as they do from the internet. I saw something on Twitter that was wide left but had some truth to it. People who were born in the mid-'80s and '90s are capable of being the most unique because they are in-between two generations—pre and post internet. I'm old enough to know what VHS tapes are and having to rewind a videotape before putting it back in its tape holder. If you go up to a random kid today, most likely, they couldn't even tell you what a VHS tape is. My grandparents believed in working hard, and my parents taught me to work smart.

Now somewhere in this silver lining, I and others must teach this younger generation how to work harder and smarter. That's the challenge. Are you willing to step up and make a difference?

As I glance at the class, I see future artists, musicians, actors, and dancers.

You recognize laughter and playfulness that only a child could have

Remembering that you were once that child trying to be the class clown

Finally, getting a chance to go to your desk and sit down

Just to have a student walk to the front of the class

And say Mr., can I get a hall pass...?

November

Either laugh or cry; because why do both? -Jemele Hill

Life after death might have been one of the greatest albums ever to be made. I like to think of this book as something of that caliber. To most, it may just be another book that was purchased to show support, and I am genuinely grateful; but do you know me? I ask this question because most don't, but if you have read this far then, you're getting a picture of the man I'm trying to be. Some will say educated, my friends will rebuttal and say I'm genuine, my family I hope would say loving, the young women who were in and out of my life will say I'm the true definition of a Scorpio; that I love hard but am distant at the same time. Growing up I feared failure, so I tried my best in simple terms to not fuck it up. Never lacked confidence; just didn't want to disappoint. The older I get, the more degrees I receive, the higher the ceiling is for me. I see my family, and I tell myself "Just don't fuck it up" I'm cursing more because I want you to feel me and to my spiritual readers I apologize for the profanity, "But he who is without sin among you, let him be the first to throw a stone."

While no longer fearing failure, I fear time because, unlike most things, you never know when your time will be finished. I tell my family and friends I love them more; I read the Bible more not because I think it will make me the perfect Christian but because it's a cheat sheet to allow you to understand that the hole you're in; many before you have come and conquered. I've known people younger than me die, so fearfulness of death is irrelevant. This segment is titled November because it's the most significant month. Time changes, seasons are beginning to change, temperatures dropping, and it gives you the most time to reflect on how much you have grown in the last year. Most will argue and say December, but once December comes, you're thinking about Christmas and how much the new year will be your best one. In a month and some change, it will be the year 2020... those of you old enough laugh because by now, you would have thought we would have flying cars, cured world hunger, and racism wouldn't exist. Yet, we wake up to student loan debt at an all-time high, an Earth dying rapidly, and mental health still going unnoticed. How can one make a difference? Truthfully, it will take all of us to participate in changing the world.

2020

January 1, 2020, the beginning of a new decade, new era, and for some a new life. It's easy to be cliché and say this will be your best year yet, but you can't claim the future if you haven't accepted the past. We can't predict the future and request to God that you want everything to fall in place if you're not able to handle the consequences that come with it. We're eight days into the new year, and one thing that strikes my eye is we as humans tend to flaunt our success yet, fathom the thought of highlighting our failures. As an author, I can tell you whatever I want about myself, and to an extent, you'll believe me. This year is all about self for me, not in a cocky way but in an expectation way. For the first time in a while, I got complacent and thought I was the smartest man in the room. Took the GMAT (Graduate Management Admission Test), and the only thing that I might have gotten correct was my name; (ahh dang I put Josh instead of Joshua on the test…) definitely failed. Make light of a situation and continue to grow to the best version of yourself. Coaching a group of young ladies has taught me that. They live in the moment, not for the future; like most millennials, I'm expecting to be a self-made millionaire who will have generational wealth. I lost focus on my health and didn't let my body receive the attention it needed. If 2020 wasn't already off to a rocky start, this would be a different pain…

Kobe

Every generation has an athlete that they hold to a compatible level of a Greek God stature, and Kobe Bryant was that individual for my generation. I write this book in real-time, so at the release of this book, this tragedy would have been about six months removed. The death of Kobe had the world in silence, and it was one of those "where were you when" moments that you will remember for the rest of your life. Even if you weren't into sports, you knew who he was. You want to embody the "Mamba" mentality in everything that you do. The first pair of shoes that I bought with my money was some red and Black "Crazy 8's" Kobe's shoe when he was signed with Adidas. I still have the shoes. Kobe left many people with expectations, something that kids growing up today lack. If you idolized this man or just respected the way he carried himself, then you at one point in time caught yourself having a mamba mentality, whether it was in an athletic setting or you just wanted to be the best that you could be. If I'm honest, I always stated I would be happy with whatever child God blessed me with, but secretly always wanted a boy. Then these highlight reels keep popping up with Kobe and his daughter; I began to realize that having a daughter would be awesome. Who wouldn't want to be a girl's dad? But I'll have to wait and see.

Corona

A global pandemic is what it is being called. There are so many emotions that I have about the coronavirus, that it will make a great story to tell the grandkids one day. Shoutout to Trump for the $1200 used to fund this book, let me stop. On a serious matter, this has been an interesting time to be alive. We have been on lockdown since late March and the States are beginning to reopen, for how long? Your guess is as good as mine. There are many things to take away from this whole crisis. The first being how wealthy the United States of America is. For weeks, we have seen countless of relief funds constructed by wealthy Americans. Which is a great thing, but my whole life on Earth there has been homeless people and citizens who had no healthcare insurance. Where were these unlimited resources?

The Trump administration was able to hand out stimulus checks to every American adult in the country who qualified for assistance. Some would say be grateful and before I go further in depth with this discussion, yes I accepted my check just like you did. My mind just has a different thought process because I began to wonder if we had this much money to assist people, why not have reparations for African American citizens? Why not be able to fix the Flint water crisis, free healthcare for everyone, but that's unrealistic. If there's any good to take from this pandemic it's the art of giving.

The biggest struggle that most people seem to have is being stuck in the house. Boredom is an obstacle, but I think people have this major fear of now having to face themselves. You find yourself being in deep thought a lot more. You're stuck at home with a spouse, family members, or sadly enough yourself. This pandemic has led up to a lot of self-reflection for myself and I hope for you. If you do not come out of this motivated to better yourself, then I'm truly sorry because you missed the whole point of this quarantine.

Joshua

I am not a recipient of your charity; you are gifted with my presence.

-Daymond John

The biggest accomplishment that I have achieved in this first half of 2020, as I write on this beautiful Sunday afternoon, is I'm human. In a society where I could have lost myself a long time ago, blessings keep reigning in and surrounding me around a support system that is second to none. Life has a funny way of showing us what's next, but I assume that is what's motivating us each day to wake up and find peace. This is who I am; the good and the bad. If College Uncensored was my breakout book, this is my homecoming. I can't take life for granted because this can be my last. I asked you, who is Joshua Hicks? That was an unfair question to ask, so I'll tell you. I am a young Black man who can code-switch with the best of them. I was fortunate enough to have an educational background that would leave most in a shock of what to be and who to be. I am an educator, a coach, a business owner, a community activist, a friend, and a son. I am a person you can walk pass every day, but if you stop... I hope to be blessed with your presence and listen to your memoir. As always, God bless.